River of Authenticity
Keys to Holy Spirit Renewal

Amos Benefield Jr.

"No man steps into the same river twice, for it is not the same river and he is not the same man." ~ Heraclitus

(River of Authenticity: Keys to Holy Spirit Renewal)
Copyright © 2017 by (Amos Benefield Jr.)

All rights reserved. No part of this book may be reproduced or transmitted in any form or by any means without written permission from the author.

Unless otherwise indicated, all Scripture quotations are taken from the Holy Bible, New International Version®, NIV®, © 1973, 1978, 1984 by the International Bible Society. Scripture quotations taken from the Amplified® Bible (AMPC), © 1954, 1958, 1962, 1964, 1965, 1987 by The Lockman Foundation Used by permission. Scripture quotations marked (KJV) are taken from the King James Version of the Holy Bible. Some definitions of Hebrew and Greek words are taken from Strong's Exhaustive Concordance. Some dictionary definitions are taken from Merriam-Webster's 11th Collegiate Dictionary and Oxford Dictionary 2nd Edition.

Lions Gate Publishing
lionsgatepublishing.org
amosbenefieldjr@yahoo.com

ISBN (13: 973-0-692-07441-1)

Table of Content

Foreword	4
Introduction	8
Chapter 1 *Chartered Streams*	10
Chapter 2 *The Restoring Rivers of Zion*	35
Chapter 3 *Cultural Assimilation*	49
Chapter 4 *The Synergistic Spiritual Development*	63
Chapter 5 *Spirit of Reformation*	76
Chapter 6 *A Paradigm Shift*	85
Chapter 7 *Glory Global*	95
Epilogue	107
Bibliography	108

Foreword

By Apostle Monroe Hodges

Apostle Amos Benefield has written a much-needed book on bringing the Glory of God's presence into the earth. The insights revealed will help you to see the hand of God through miracles, healing, deliverance and breakthrough.

I highly recommend this resource to anyone who has a hunger and thirst for a real move of God in their life, family, church, or community. Read this book, apply the principles, and experience an open Heaven that can only come through fervent prayer.

Apostle Monroe Hodges
City of God Church

Foreword
By Dr. Jason Jackson

While simultaneously serving as the principal of a progressive investment bank and a full time senior pastor I am consistently pulled between the seen and unseen worlds. When rationale seeks to drive my conclusions, my faith in the unseen GOD compels me alternatively. As such, after three decades of consideration I've arrived at the conclusion that what is witnessed in the natural world is only a mere manifestation of what has prevailed in the immaterial world. The River of Authenticity serves as a distinct guide to understanding the prevailing world of the supernatural.

By challenging contemporary misunderstandings of Christian faith, Apostle Benefield does not distort Christian teaching, but draws upon often unnoticed currents of theology which are often discolored by established religious leaders. The author's own experience presents this book a stamp of authenticity. He speaks, not as a bystander, but as a practitioner. For more than twenty years, Apostle Benefield has operated within the confines of supernatural ministry, and what his writing has been forged with is an anvil. This is a refreshing read.

It is relevant. It is spiritually motivating. It is naturally provoking. One looking for new ways to fulfill the Great Commission of authentically presenting the heart of Jesus will find it here. With joy, I commend it to you.

Dr. Jason Jackson
Chairman & Founder
Jackson Global Initiative
Forbes Finance Council Member

Foreword
By Bishop Christopher C. Smith

We are living in the days that we see much compromise. If we are really honest with ourselves, it is everywhere we look. Compromise is found in our nation's capital, our court houses, our school systems, and even in many of our churches.

The Bible says, "If our foundation be destroyed, what can the righteous do?" (Psalm 11:3) Our nation and our institutions of education were built on the foundation of Christianity. However, today we see men in positions of leadership exalting their knowledge above the knowledge of God. When did the creation become wiser than its Creator?

Many have turned from serving the only true and living God solely to become self-serving. Many of our churches have even watered down their messages and the true move of the Spirit of God to get people to feel more comfortable in their services. I don't believe God intended the church to create an atmosphere of comfort, as much as I believe He intended the church to create an atmosphere where He can dwell, and people can be changed. Why would we ever settle for the cheaper when God has given us access to the deeper? I believe the deep is calling to the deep once again. Our nation and many churches are dehydrated and are in need of a real awakening, but there cannot be an awakening until people turn their hearts back to God and drink from the fountain of living water.

Apostle Amos Benefield masterfully lays out, what I call, a roadmap that leads his readers back to the heart of God by creating a true hunger and thirst for a real move of God. By themselves, men cannot create an authentic move of God. We can hold meetings every year and invite the best, prolific speakers from around the world, but that does not necessarily mean that these are all the right ingredients for an authentic move that gives birth to revival. You may be blessed, but that does not necessarily mean you are in the atmosphere of a genuine move of God. All we can do as men is repair the soul of our hearts through prayer, sowing, and watering; it is God who gives the increase. In other words, men cannot create a real revival; it is God who decides to move in the hearts of His people when we meet His conditions. We cannot meet God's conditions until every hindrance is removed out of our lives. That is when our broken fellowship with God will be restored.

In this book, Apostle Amos Benefield captures some of the greatest moves of God over the course of many generations. You will discover that those who God used in their day to usher in an authentic move of God were not pursuing a revival, they were pursuing God. They were not trying to make names for themselves or get people to attend their meetings; they were simply trying to meet God's conditions. It was through their own passion and pursuit to discover who God really is that their fire caused others of the same like-mindedness to be ignited with passion, hunger, and a thirst to drink from the Master's well. May the *River Of Authenticity* cause you to become spiritually renewed and create a hunger and thirst in you to pursue what matters most, an authentic move of God. Now, come and drink from the river that never runs dry.

Bishop Christopher C Smith, D.D.
In Him Embassy Ministries
New Destiny Church
Global Apostolic Council

Introduction
Holy Spirit Come!

"The Spirit and the bride say, "Come!" And let the one who hears say, "Come!" Let the one who is thirsty come; and let the one who wishes take the free gift of the water of life." ~ Revelation 22:17

From the beginning of creation, the Holy Spirit's objective has been to saturate the planet with His glorious presence. Although the forces of darkness have fought to keep the cosmos in bleak obscurity, creation constantly yearns for the Glory of God. This divine appeal is from Jesus Christ and His bride, who simultaneously cries out to the whole of humanity.

This invitation is for all who are spiritually thirsty for Heaven's release to leave their places of dormancy and restraints, return to the God of all creation, and be filled with His glorious presence. Certainly, this was the same passionate cry that gave birth to past moves of God; an awakening that would eventually start the third wave of glory.

Today, we are in a dimensional shift in the 21st century church age. The moral compass of the world has influenced Christianity in so much that there is a dire need for clarity and spiritual renewal. Society at-large is so desperate for the supernatural until many are even seeking it through the Paranormal. Nevertheless, as it was in the Genesis of times, the Spirit of God is hovering over the Earth and moving upon the waters again!

The time is far spent and the beckoning hour is at hand, to wake up and be adorned in the apparel of light. The wedding feast has been prepared, but the bride must realign her heart with the bridegroom's and prepare for His glorious return.

River of Authenticity will help you to navigate the former moves of the Holy Spirit that literally impacted the world. From their stages of infancy to the current flow of the Holy Spirit in the now. You will be informed of what were the virtues that gave birth to literal outpourings and spiritual awakenings and the things that challenged their momentum. Also, it addresses the urgent need of the restoration of the Spirit and to inspire you to have a greater desire for the presence of God. In addition, the book is geared towards provoking the God Chasers into a deeper and more intimate quest for Him and to compel them to live on the extreme end for His kingdom and glory.

Chapter One
Chartered Streams

"Oh, that you, Almighty God, would rend the heavens, that you would come down, that the mountains might shake at Your presence."
~ Isaiah 64:1

What Is Revival?

In the most simplified terms, revival is when humanity has an encounter with God and is supernaturally transformed. It is a great privilege to live in a country like America, where there is free choice and religion. However, the only thing that can revitalize the human spirit is a sovereign move of God. It is impossible to have such an encounter and not be forever changed.

Whenever God reveals Himself to humanity, life is restored to the lifeless and hope lives in the hopeless. The spiritual deadness of a worldly culture will always require a solemn act of God.

It must be realized that presidents and governmental strategies are incapable of restoring the tarnished soil of a society who has morally strayed away from God.

In terms of society at large, the state of the church is the compass that will generally determine its social and moral conditions. With this said, revival has a vital part to play and has tremendous global impact. Revival is a great necessity for restoring nations, because of the supernatural effect that is has on the world. Marriages are strengthened, families are restored, and people are healed and filled with God's Spirit as a result of it.

Unfortunately, many churches today are only gathering places filled with souls that are spiritually starving. Programs and religious jargon has filled the pews but has failed to meet the needs of those who long for spiritual renewal. This is why it is so necessary that people understand the importance of true revival.

Revival is not a series of church services that are put together for the sole purpose of being emotionally aroused. Revival is not a gathering that is held seasonally with the intent to save a few souls. Revival is when God rends the Heavens and invades time with eternity. Revival radically transforms the hearts of humanity.

In chartering the past moves of the Spirit within the last 100 years, you will discover that the spirit of revival came with an intense force of winds that literally broke religious and social barriers and proposed new paradigms for Christians who sought for the fullness of God. The past moves of God were initiated by nothing less than an unquenchable, ever longing for the heart of God. Eventually, this caused spiritual awakenings, which transformed men and women and would be transferred from one generation to another. This was literally Heavens response to the crescendos cry of humanity.

The outpouring of the past would come like supernatural rivers that would gain great momentum, diminishing and then starting again with the preceding generation. The carriers of these mighty outpourings would glean from the fame and reputation of the former ones. Earnest desperation and an overwhelming desire to see the

Supernatural power of God demonstrated on Earth is what caused this.

Now, the hour has come for the restitution and recovery of global revival!

Charismatic Christianity

Every outpouring of the past impressed indubitable earmarks on Christians who would thereafter be called Charismatics. The word Charismatic comes from the word Charisma, denoting grace gifts and extraordinary powers.

According to a study conducted by The Pew Research Center[1], Christianity makes up at least 70% of the population's religion. Although this is a high percentile, many who claim Christianity today will sing and talk about the Jesus of History but would not dare testify that He can do what He did in the four Gospels. In fact, Jesus openly said to His disciples in Saint John chapter fourteen verse twelve:

"Verily, verily, I say unto you, He that believeth on me, the works that I do shall he do also; and greater works than these shall he do; because I go unto my Father." ~ John 14:12

---

[1] "Religious Study Landscape," accessed August 19, 2017. http://www.pewforum.org/religious-landscape-study/.

However, today when you begin to talk about the idea of greater works, miracles and wonders, or even being Fascinated and captivated by God's presence, people look at you like you have a third eye in the middle of your forehead. There are many religious people today who settle for Mundane Christianity, void of God's power. An authentic charismatic believer generally will emphasize on the works of the Holy Spirit. Today, there are many evangelicals who only focus on the historical God of the Bible and never allow Him to go beyond the pages of the Old and New Testament.

Ignorance of God's ability to move today is one thing that may express a lack of knowledge about Him. However, when we have been biblically informed that He is the same today, yesterday, and forevermore, then there should be no denying of His operative power in the now. Furthermore, when the proof of His existence manifests itself daily in creation, there should be no reason to doubt His existence or capabilities.

Today, there are many religious preferences and professions that are void of actual proof of God's power. Often, people religiously claim their faith by nomenclature alone when the dividing line of one's belief should be based on their conviction and evidence. I am sure that many inquiring minds would like to know the meaning of nomenclature.

Nomenclature is defined as the act, process, or an instance of naming things. Though names have great importance, and should reveal character and purpose, on the contrary, it is not always the case. It does not necessarily mean that something or someone is authentic. For example, just because a person calls themselves a Christian does not necessarily mean that they bear the earmarks of a true believer. In fact, many call themselves Christians, but do not even have a conviction for Christ, let alone, a burden for the lost.

Nowadays, people dare to say that they are believers, but do not believe in divine healing or the idea that miracles even exist. In fact, in our times, many Christian leaders are settling for being called life coaches and motivational speakers and have relegated the gospel message to merely the power of positive thinking, rather than the message of the cross and real faith in God for the supernatural.

"And these signs shall follow them that believe; In my name shall they cast out devils; they shall speak with new tongues;" ~ Mark 16:17

Charismatic believers will normally allow gifts of the Spirit to freely flow. Faith, fervent prayer, and prophecy are strong attributes of Charismatic, Spirit-Filled believers. The Holy Spirit Enlightened Charismatic Movement was originally birthed out of Pentecostalism, which goes all the way back to the birthing of the New Testament Church. One out of every four Christian believers is documented as being Pentecostal and/or Charismatic[2]. It is factual that God will always use people as conduits to demonstrate His power

---

[2] Marc Cortez, "The Growth of Global Pentecostalism," *Everyday Theology* (Blog), April 14, 2014, http://marccortez.com/2014/04/16/growth-global-pentecostalism-wheaton-theology-conference-4/.

In fact, the evidence of this can be traced even in the lives of the patriarchs in the Old and New Testament. For example, in Exodus chapter nine verse one; God used Moses' stammering tongue to command the release of the children of Israel with miraculous wonders following Him. In Joshua chapter ten verse thirteen, Joshua prayed for the sun to stand still, and the Bible says that the sun and moon stayed still for a whole day until Israel had avenge themselves of their enemies. In 1 and 2 Kings, Elijah and Elisha were very charismatic in character by both having a tremendous display of the miraculous in their ministries.

Although the display of God's power can be discovered throughout the Bible, in modern times true Charismatics generally will focus on the vivid display of God's power and not just relate to it as only Bible stories. This will be discussed further in later chapters.

Prayer is what fuels revival fire and charismatic renewal. This is vital and must be understood. Any move of the Holy Spirit will lose its intensity when the contenders attempt to only duplicate the prior moves. What I mean by this is, though we honor the forerunners and revivals of the past, we must not make them to be mere monuments. We must understand that it is not enough to repeat them but realize that they all had their individual cause and purpose to their generation.

It is amazing that after two thousand years, many people are still waiting for another Pentecost when actually the church will never see that move again because, that window has closed. I would like to clearly reiterate that there can never be another Pentecost like the first one, because originally it was the signature of a new dispensation.

However, despite this truth, every person who receives the Holy Spirit initially can receive Him in the fullness just like they did in the Book of Acts.

To further explain, what the glorious church should be anticipating right now is a move of the Spirit that will precede the ones that have already came! Without a doubt the former outpourings were more than just occurrences, but they were divine encounters from Heaven. As a result of the relentless search for the God of all creation, a gravitational pull from the Earth provoke the Heavens to respond with refreshing springs of revival. The outpouring of the Holy Spirit took on many different characteristics, such as transforming winds, refreshing springs, and rivers of fires; that changed people's lives forever.

Here are some monumental outpourings that astonishingly marked church history in ways that can never be erased.

The Birthing of Fire[3]
William Seymour and the Apostolic Faith Mission

"And I saw as it were a sea of glass mingled with fire: and them that had gotten the victory over the beast, and over his image, and over his mark, and over the number of his name, stand on the sea of glass, having the harps of God." ~Rev 15:2

---

[3] "The Azusa Street Revival", Apostolic Archives International, accessed August 19, 2017.
http://www.apostolicarchives.com/articles/article/8801925/173190.htm.

In 1906, the people in Los Angeles, California experienced an uncontrollable fire that would last for several years. This amazing phenomenon was called the *Azusa Street Revival*. This revival gained such a reputation that it literally impacted the nations of the world. William J. Seymour, an African-American preacher, spearheaded the revival. Seymour was the pastor of the Apostolic Faith Mission Church. Seymour and his followers' original intentions were not to give birth to a movement; rather, they were desperately seeking the presence and power of God. This search ignited the spark of this tumultuous outpouring of the Holy Spirit.

The Azusa Street Revival started in a small building on 216 North Bonnie Brae Street, where people of different racial backgrounds would gather and pray to receive the baptism of the Holy Spirit. In an article published by *The Apostolic Archives*, it was documented that after around ten days of fervent prayer and passionately crying out to God, He broke out amongst the people and baptized and filled them with His Holy Spirit. These meetings grew so expeditiously that they had to find another place to hold them. Eventually, they moved to a new location, which was an old abandoned building that was formally an African Methodist Episcopal Church on Azusa Street. Little did the contenders know that this would end up being an encounter that would not only mark that generation but would also signature history and successively carry the spirit of revival from nation to nation. Although devout Christians and sceptics came to Azusa, most of the people who were in attendance were sincerely and extremely desperate for God.

"Then shall ye call upon me, and ye shall go and pray unto me, and I will hearken unto you. And ye shall seek me, and find me, when ye shall search for me with all your heart." Jer 29;12

When God is found by men, He cannot be contained. When men search for God out of a deep desire for Him, His glory will be their reward. This is exactly what happened in this great revival. These God Chasers sought Him intensely until He manifested Himself to them. This move of the Holy Spirit had built a tremendous momentum and gained great notoriety.

Similar to the first Pentecost in Acts,

"There appear to them tongues resembling fire were distributed among them, and they rested on each one of them [as each person received the Holy Spirit]. And they were all filled [that is, diffused throughout their being] with the Holy Spirit and began to speak in other tongues (different languages), as the Spirit was giving them the ability to speak out [clearly and appropriately]"

~ Acts 2:3-4

I am sure the attendees in 1906 were praying to have experience like the Pentecost experience Acts 2, just as many Christians around the globe today are praying to experience another outpouring like Azusa. There is absolutely nothing wrong with wanting to duplicate something good. The success of the Azusa Street Revival can be used as a model. However, the despairing cry of the hearts of men today should not be repetitive, but our plea should be: *"Lord, take us further than our fathers!"*

Lord give us more of you!

The manifest presence of God drew crowds of thousands. Many people were baptized in the Holy Spirit with the evidence of speaking in tongues. God's presence and power among them was so strong that it broke barriers and became interracially woven. This was during the Jim Crow Era of racial segregation, yet the crowds were culturally diverse. Although the residue of slavery in America was very much present, the desire for the heart of God was even stronger and it was the common factor in bringing the contenders together.

It is documented that thousands visited Azusa to experience it firsthand. Many people received impartations and brought them to other nations. As the Azusa Street Revival had taken on the characteristics of the prophecy of Joel chapter two, many people left Azusa and became missionaries in remote areas of the world. It is documented that missionaries went forth in Africa, Kolcutta, India, Hong Kong, North China, etc. Many people were strongly influenced by this sovereign move.

Within two years, the movement had spread to over fifty nations. Leaders came to visit from all over the world.

Many Spirit-Filled denominations were birthed out of The Azusa Street Revival, which are still alive today. The revival on Azusa Street lasted from 1906 until 1915.

The Welsh Awakening[4]

While the birthing of fire was taking place in the United States, a very powerful awakening had already begun in the United Kingdom called The Welsh Awakening.

During the spring of 1904, a young Welshman by the name of Evan Roberts would awaken early every morning and meet with God for several hours. Roberts was an astounding gentleman who was relentless in his pursuit for God. He was not aware that his hunger for God would end up literally drawing that nation to Christ.

This was the largest Christian revival in Wales during the 20th century. Its force had a great effect on that entire region. Churches were literally filled for two decades because of this revival. The rest of Great Britain and other parts of the globe also experienced its thrust. Missionaries from Great Britain were sent to Africa, Latin America and other nations to spiritually awaken those regions of the world.

The Welsh Awakening even impacted South Korea, who was so impacted by the message of salvation, that a vast majority of their society was converted into Christianity[5]. The South Korean church experienced phenomenal growth as a result of God revealing Himself to that nation. Now, in that region, Christians make up 29%

of its population.

Yoido Full Gospel Church in Seoul Korea[6]

In 1958, the Yoido Full Gospel Church in Seoul Korea was founded and led by David Yonggi Cho. It had the largest Christian congregation in South Korea, and the world, with the acclaimed estimation of over 800,000 members. Even though Wales was the catalyst for the revival that broke out in Korea, it has now shifted and is no longer a major carrier of revival today as it was in the early 1900s. A census was taken that amazingly revealed 32%[7] of the people in Wales claim that they do not belong to a religious group. Today, Wales is known for its increasing rate of suicide among teens[8] and occultism[9], which has become an alluring trend in that region of the world.

---

[4] "Evan Roberts", God's Generals, accessed August 19, 2017. http://godsgenerals.com/evanroberts.

[5] Vance Christie, "When Revival Came To Korea" last modified May 21, 2015. http://www.vancechristie.com/2015/05/21/when-revival-came-to-korea/.

[6] Lucky Severson, "World's Biggest Congregation" last modified August 10, 2012. http://www.pbs.org/wnet/religionandethics/2012/08/10/august-10-2012-worlds-biggest-congregation/10162/

[7] "Census 2011: One-Third in Wales Have No Religion," *BBC News,* last modified December 11, 2012. http://www.bbc.com/news/uk-wales-20678136.

[8] Rod Nordland, "A Welsh Teen Suicide Epidemic" modified February 28, 2008. http://www.newsweek.com/welsh-teen-suicide-epidemic-94011

[9] "Witchcraft Thriving In The Welsh Countryside," *Telegraph*, last modified December 31, 2012. http://www.telegraph.co.uk.

Although the Welsh Awakening ended in 1905, its great impact last for at least 20 years.

The Healing Revivals[10]

There's a movement that emerged in America in 1947 called *The Voice of Healing*. Many great men and women of God were raised up during this era who demonstrated the Supernatural power of God in their times.

These were major key holders of the winds, fire, and springs of revival. Great generals like William Branham, Jack Cole, A.A. Allen, C.S. Upthegrove, and Oral Roberts, were some of the few that were raised up by God who greatly demonstrated His power to that generation and many came behind them.

The Voice of Healing Movement was so great that a magazine was published by Gordon Lindsey, entitled the *Voice of Healing Magazine*, in honor of the movement. The magazine chronicled the mighty acts and infallible proofs of the Holy Spirit and the phenomenal things that occurred in those camp meetings during the movement. Many of these great voices touch generations; and although, some of the patriarchs fell into areas of deception, it did not stop God's presence and power from being displayed in the lives of

---

[10] Tony Cauchi, "Overview of The Healing Revival" last modified date September 2011. http://www.voiceofhealing.info

those who were spiritually hungry for Him.

In 1958, The Voice of Healing Movement ended. It's said that some of the contenders fell in certain areas, yet great deliverance was still brought to many people. Unfortunately, sometimes the very people who are called to be carriers of great moves of God can end up getting caught in the snare of deception. Some people make the mistake of forgetting that they human and not divine.

Please understand, this is something that should never be taken lightly, because they are demonic assignments against any sovereign move of the Spirit. Sin, deception, and religious dogma can lessen or even put to halt the move of the Holy Spirit.

This is an important truth. When people start claiming entitlement to what belongs to God, they will easily get snared into the trap of deception. Whenever servants of God get full of themselves, they will eventually end up deceiving themselves and others.

Understanding God's sovereignty is the key to sustainability and having His trust. Sovereignty is having supreme authority and the full rights over a governing body to govern it without any interference. Understanding that God governs everything by His own sovereignty and will is very vital for the move of the Holy Spirit. He is supreme and has total preeminence over everything. Human interference will only place caps and restrictions on the flow of God and can bring a hindrance to His plans and purposes. Whenever

Carnality and calamity intermingles with divinity,
divine purposes are prohibited from being established.

People who are not sensitive to the Holy Spirit will hinder the moves of the Holy Spirit. Being sensitive to the Holy Spirit is key to maximizing windows of Heaven. However, when people struggle with power, they become intoxicated with themselves and will not be able to handle upward mobility. But what is a greater travesty is when other people are hindered by their incongruent behavior.

When a person stands at the cusp of something great, designed by God and are responsible for progressing it, but get caught up, they can easily end up causing a catastrophe to it. Without discretion and humility, much power can bring corruption. Vain glory causes an offense to a true move of the Spirit every time. In the Bible, there were certain kings who this happened to. They were arrogant and eventually fell into sin. For example, King Belshazzar and King Saul were kings who were prideful and misjudged God's sovereignty.

"And thou his son, O Belshazzar, hast not humbled thine heart, though thou knewest all this; But hast lifted up thyself against the Lord of heaven; and they have brought the vessels of his house before thee, and thou, and thy lords, thy wives, and thy concubines, have drunk wine in them; and thou hast praised the gods of silver, and gold, of brass, iron, wood, and stone, which see not, nor hear, nor

> *know: and the God in whose hand thy breath is, and whose are all thy ways, hast thou not glorified:" ~ Daniel 5:22-23*

King Belshazzar's fall in leadership came through sins of omission, which is to know to do right but refused to do it. Belshazzar was a king who was prideful and disregarded God. Also, King Saul was guilty of being arrogant and very stubborn in his leadership.

> *For rebellion is as the sin of witchcraft, and stubbornness is as iniquity and idolatry. Because thou hast rejected the word of the LORD, he hath also rejected thee from being king.*
>
> *~ I Samuel 15:23*

King Saul was so arrogant, instead of asking God's forgiveness for his pride and arrogance in *I Samuel 15: 30*, he chose to overlook his issue, expecting God to bless him anyway. I think this often happens today.

It is important to address this, when God's presence is pursued, He often transmits His power through human beings, which often comes with the test of pride. Staying grounded is always contingent upon people maintaining humility and remaining mentally and spiritually sober. If a person desires to be a carrier of God's presence, they must never be confused over who the power source really is. He or She must never be mistaken as to who is using who!

Contenders of Gods glorious presence should ask themselves this very important question; *"Is God using me, or am I using Him?"* You would be amazed at how many people today use their gifts to fulfill their own selfish appetites.

By all means, spiritual elevation is a great thing, but people will struggle in this area if they do not equally understand the importance of being grounded. Whenever this starts occurring, it is a clear indication that one's ascension is on its way to an abrupt descent.

Sometimes, what is more important than how high you can fly, is how long can you soar? Soaring to heights can be a wonderful experience, but it is impossible to sustain the flow of gravitation without the laws of motion. Newton's first law of motion is applied to, or, is the basis of aviation[11]. This principle is called, *The Law of Lift*. Every pilot must understand this to successfully fly an airplane. Without the law of lift, the pilot will never experience upward mobility. This same rule can be applied to every glory carrier. The same law that lift's you must be the same one to sustain you. Those who refuse to maintain the law of elevation will eventually succumb to another law called *Crash and Burn*.

Think about this:

---

[11] Nancy Hall, "Newton's First Law," last modified May 5, 2015. https://www.grc.nasa.gov/www/k-12/airplane/newton1.html

An airplane should never leave the runway under these conditions:

1. Mechanical Failure
2. An Unhealthy Pilot
3. A Pilot Under the Influence

Likewise, people who aspire to be used of God should think in the same manner.

It is impossible to remain ascended if you are dysfunctional. Whenever a person is full of self, they are not healthy enough to lead anyone into a sovereign move of the Holy Spirit. And will eventually end up putting people lives in danger. When people are puffed up in leadership, they will easily fall into a spirit of error and eventually become dogmatic. Before you know it, they will have left behind path of destruction.

Dogmatic, deceptive leadership behavior should never be at the forefront of an advancing move of God. Deception and religious dogma have always been weapons the enemy has used to cause dysfunction in the Body of Christ. This is a great hindrance to the progressive moves of the Holy Spirit. When a man's ways are dogmatic it can easily hinder what God is doing. Many movements have lost their mobility because of this issue.

Dogma, which is the root word for dogmatic, is a set of principles laid down by a person in authority as incontrovertibly true, serving as the primary basis of the belief system which cannot be changed, challenged, or discarded. When people are dogmatic, they only see things one way and are unwilling to accept anything else as truth, even when there is actual proof of it.

Dogmatic behavior is one of the very things that has caused separation in the Lord's Church and has reduced the river of the Spirit from flowing in certain places. This is what causes radical, on fire, movements to become religiously starch and void the transforming power of the Holy Spirit.

Despite of this, God is persistent in showing Himself to the coming generations. The momentum of many past moves ceased because of the forces, which opposed them, as well as the inability of the carriers to sustain the force. But just as waves are created by energy which passes through the ocean, in circular motion; likewise, the currents of revival will somehow always flow from generation to generation.

The Pensacola Outpouring[12]

In the late 1900s, something stirred in the heavens. The River was released again. This time the visitation was in Pensacola Florida where the *Pensacola Outpouring* was birthed.

---

[12] "Honoring the Past," Brownsville Assembly of God, accessed August 19, 2017. http://brownsville.church/about-us/history.

For several years, Pastor John Philpatrick and his members were contending in prayer for revival to come to their church in Pensacola, Florida. On June 18, 1995, the inevitable happened. What was supposed to be a camp meeting at Brownsville Assembly of God Church did not conclude until five years later. The leaders of this church had prayed and planned for years for revival to come. When it came, it lingered for years. From Wednesday to Saturday evenings, the church was filled with people crying out and worshiping God. Night after night, during altar calls, people would fill the altars and give their lives to Jesus Christ.

In search of a true move of God, people would travel across the world just to experience Him at the Pensacola Outpouring. The Brownsville Church states, *"worshipers from nearly every continent flocked to the West Pensacola suburb of Brownsville to receive a touch from the Father."*

The Contenders of Glory[13]

In 1994, a great portal opened over Toronto Canada, people at the Toronto Airport Vineyard Church began to experience supernatural waves of Glory. British newspapers would later call this phenomenon the *Toronto Blessing*. Pastors John and Carol Arnott invited Apostle Randy Clark of St. Louis, Missouri to minister at their church.

---

[13] John Arnott, "The Toronto Blessing: What Is It?," last modified December 31, 1999. http://www.johnandcarol.org/updates/the-toronto-blessing-what-is-it.

It is recorded that their first meeting had about one hundred twenty people in attendance. By the first year, the church membership had increased in such a way that their original location had become too small, causing them to relocate to a conference hall which accommodated four thousand people.

The Vineyard Church was known for spiritual ecstasy and the leaders were gatekeepers of this profound move of the Holy Spirit. The people at the church placed no restriction on the Holy Spirit and the supernatural power of God. Just like any other glory carriers, they were mocked and criticized for the movement, but it did not stop them from being contenders of charismatic renewal. In fact, the Toronto Airport Church, which is now called *Catch the Fire*, is still very much known for its supernatural manifestations. Today, people still travel from all over the world *to Jump in the River* at *Catch the Fire*.

Now, we are in the 21st century, at the cusp of the next wave of glory. Just as it were with the former moves of God, certain things must take precedence to set the stage for latter glory encounters. There are certain principles and prerequisites that can never be overlooked.

Keys to Renewal

There were two things that were responsible for Heaven's release in the former moves of God. They were:

1. Desperation

2. Intercession

Desperation

Discussed through this book, desperation is a key requirement for taping into the heart of God. It is the key requirement for past and present moves of God. When it comes to the relentless quest, desperation is a must. It is a major key to taping into Heaven's access.

When you are not desperately seeking God, it is difficult to experience the things of God. Those who desperately pursue His face will eventually have His heart. Having desperation causes a deeper longing of the soul to know God in such a way until one's heart is filled with a deep passion for Him. True desperation will expose the purity of one's heart and reveal their true hunger and thirst.

Blessed are they which do hunger and thirst after righteousness: for they shall be filled.

~ Matthew 5:6

Intercession

When it comes to intercession, many people have fallen short; not realizing that it is more than just mundane praying. Real intercession requires passion and spiritual stamina. In other words, true intercession will require the heart and strength to pray something all the way through.

This can be compared to a woman in labor. She will travail until she has given birth.

People who do not develop a prayer life will never develop the spiritual stamina to birth something out in the realm of the Spirit.

Who hath heard such a thing? who hath seen such things? Shall the earth be made to bring forth in one day? or shall a nation be born at once? for as soon as Zion travailed, she brought forth her children. Shall I bring to the birth, and not cause to bring forth? saith the LORD: shall I cause to bring forth, and shut the womb? saith thy God.

~ Isaiah 66:8-9

Spiritual labor pains are an indication that what you are carrying in the spiritual womb, you'll soon give birth to.

I reiterate, giving birth to spiritual things, will require stamina. This is the reason why people lack answers from God and remain destitute of power with Him, this is the result of not developing a prayer life.

The keys to successful intercession are both faith and stamina. They are synonymous.

But without faith it is impossible to please him: for he that cometh to God must believe that he is, and that he is a rewarder of them that diligently seek him. ~ Hebrews 11:6

There are many Christians who have experienced spiritual miscarriages and aborted purposes, because they never learned how to faithfully travail in prayer. In fact, these forces birth movements and are the catalyst for charismatic renewal. However, pride and arrogance will demobilize and cause spiritual paralysis. These behaviors will minimize the flow of the spirit and relegate it to something fleshy and ineffective. For instance, when pride and arrogance is detected in leadership, leaders will:

1. Refuse to accept they are wrong.
2. Refuse to repent.
3. Refuse to listen to council.
4. Succumb to a spirit of error.

Understand this, pride and arrogance are detrimental to the sovereign moves of the Spirit, but prayer, faith and spiritual stamina will cause true revival to flow from the heart.

Highlights

In Chapter One, certain things were advantageous that fueled the outpourings of the past and are vital to our times, like desperation and prayer. Pride and arrogance are major assassins that were against past moves of God.

Transitional Prayer

Father, I passionately pursue after you; consume me in your presence. Give me a spirit of humility and deliver me from all pride and arrogance. I confess you are the sovereign Lord alone and that there is no glory in my flesh.

I submit my entire being to you; spirit, soul, and body. I examine myself and I ask you to take away all mental and spiritual contamination. Give me a willing heart and wash me thoroughly in the river of truth and righteousness!

In the name of your dear son Jesus Christ. Amen!

Chapter Two
The Restoring Rivers of Zion

> "Repent ye therefore, and be converted, that your sins may be blotted out, when the times of refreshing shall come from the presence of the Lord." ~ Acts 3:19

The church, especially in the western parts of the world, is guilty of becoming narcissistic and falling in love with herself.

The only hope for true reformation is that the blinders of loath-fullness are taken off and she returns to her first love! The Refreshing River of the Spirit must first flow from Zion, the church, and then permeate the Earth. However, returning to love is the first Clarion Call for the restoration of Zion's pure river. When Zion gets an understanding of the Father's love, it will cause a spirit of repentance to come and the fruits of grace will be the result of it. This will come with a fresh revelation of the Father's love. His grace will progressively move the church further, so that we will no longer be held hostage in the waters of imperfection. With this said, when it comes to the message of grace today, we are in need of great clarity and understanding...

Understanding the Grace Zone

"For the grace of God that bringeth salvation hath appeared to all men, teaching us that, denying ungodliness and worldly lusts, we should live soberly, righteously, and godly, in this present world" Titus 2;11,12

In the most accurate term, grace is God's riches at Christ expense. To simplify it, grace is God's unmerited favor. But many today are stretching the grace of God out of context.

In Christendom, there are many believers who have embraced the message of grace in a sense of carnal acceptance. Many people are adapting to an attitude of, *"I'm okay, you're okay and we're all okay, because Jesus died for our sins, making them none and void."* This is a great deception!

In the western society, one of the first mentioning of grace is learned in childhood. Most of us were taught this before eating a meal. It is there where we learned to say our grace:

"God is Grace. God is good. God, we thank you for our food."

"Let us therefore come boldly unto the throne of grace, that we may obtain mercy, and find grace to help in time of need." ~ *Hebrews 4:16*

However, grace is not about having gratitude about what God has done or imperfection acceptance. Neither, is it a license to sin or passport to do whatever inconceivably imagined. The grace of God not only pardons, but perfects. The grace of God graces the believer to live proportionate with God's will which teaches us to reject ungodliness and worldly (immoral) desires, and to live sensible, upright, and godly lives – lives with a purpose which reflect spiritual maturity- in this present age.

I thank God for the many teachings of grace today. However, when vain philosophies take the context of God's word and relegate it to pretext alone, it keeps people from growing spiritually. When people believe that grace has covered everything at Calvary, including unconfessed, un repented sin, then they will remain bound to a life of bondage and will never experience true liberty in the Spirit.

Of course, grace covers, but it also enables a person to live a triumphant life in Christ. Hyper grace teaching has become very trendy today; it is not only popular in western society but abroad. The problem with this kind of teaching is it does not require repentance or any holy standard of living. Grace in its totality is not unmerited favor alone, but it is from the inside out.

The Inward Workings of Grace

What the world teaches is freedom of choice and self-will, but the truth of the matter is, we can't do anything without God's enablement. People must learn to totally yield their lives to Him, and then and only then, will they discover the inward workings of grace.

Who is Grace?

Grace is Christ and the inner witness of grace is the Holy Spirit. He is the governor of grace from the inside out.

"But ye are not in the flesh, but in the Spirit, if so be that the Spirit of God dwell in you. Now if any man has not the Spirit of Christ, he is none of his."

~ Romans 8:9

This scripture helps us to understand the importance of the Holy Spirit. Without the Holy Spirit operating within us, we are not partakers of His grace, which governs from the inside out. In fact, the only proof of us being His Spiritual offspring is His grace working in our innermost being.

> *"I will open rivers in high places, and fountains in the midst of the valleys: I will make the wilderness a pool of water, and the dry land springs of water."*
> *~ Isaiah 41:18*

This scripture is a direct message to the Church. The rivers of the Holy Spirit must be opened in the high places first! Here is a good question. How can the rivers flow in the valley, when the streams are clogged up in the high places? In other words, how can the world be impacted by the times of refreshing, when the church is on life support? Revival starts with the church and its leadership, before it can truly have an impact on the world.

True Succession

When the refreshing river flows from Zion, it will permeate the Earth with God's presence. Those who will maturely sustain its flow will experience true apostolic succession.

The succession of any sovereign move of the Spirit will lose its authenticity if the fundamental value and virtues are lost. When the credibility of anything is lost, it is hard for it to rightfully serve its intended purpose.

It is very important for people to realize that what they are becoming should have everything to do with how they adapt to growth, development, and change. A

Individual successively maturing is based on the same truth. Although the Bible documents the empowerment of the church over two thousand years ago, keeping its credibility in a consistent changing society is vital. For this reason, preserving its authenticity is something that is very important, that should be passed down.

> *"And it shall come to pass in the last days, saith God, I will pour out of my Spirit upon all flesh: and your sons and your daughters shall prophesy, and your young men shall see visions, and your old men shall dream dreams: And on my servants and on my handmaidens, I will pour out in those days of my Spirit; and they shall prophesy:"*
>
> *~ Acts 2:17-18*

The difference between *Acts 2* and any other book in the Bible is it was the initial birthing of the New Testament Church. The first outpouring of the Holy Spirit majorly impacted people who were from many nationalities who gathered in Jerusalem. This was not a mere coming together, but it was a divine appointment. It was not just another gathering, but it was a Clarion Call to a *Kairos* Moment! This monumental multicultural gathering sealed the future of the church for the worlds to come.

"And, behold, I send the promise of my Father upon you: but tarry ye in the city of Jerusalem, until ye be endued with power from on high."
~ Luke 24:49

The apostles' obedience to the directive given by Jesus literally influenced the apostolic succession of the church.

In *Acts 2:17*, Apostle Peter's announcement was the fulfillment of the prophetic word spoken by Joel the Prophet in *Joel 2:28*. The fulfillment of the prophecy has impacted generations and will affect generations to come. When the decree was made concerning sons and daughters, it depicted the first recipients who received the outpouring of the Spirit. This was more than just about the outpouring, but rather, a higher calling. The apostles were not a bunch of hippies who were looking for the next spiritual craze, but they were recipients of the original move of the Spirit. From *Acts 2,* a declaration of an apostolic and prophetic generation impacted and transformed generations to come, but it also exposes illegitimacy.

When believers are trusted to walk in the supernatural, they are the true children of God, exhibiting in them the true character and nature of Him. The deep things of God should never be placed in the hands of those who are immature. Super divine earmarks and glory encounters can only be sustained in the lives of those who have embraced the process of becoming mature ones.

> *"Beloved, now are we the sons of God, and it doth not yet appear what we shall be: but we know that, when he shall appear, we shall be like him; for we shall see him as he is." ~ I John 3:2*

The church must gain a greater understanding of Son ship. Son ship is the key to dominion and authority. However, the price of true dominion and authority is maturation. Immaturity leads to carnality. When people are carnal, they will not respond to the beckoning call of the Holy Spirit.

Every outpouring of the Holy Spirit begins with mature sons and daughters of God. Now concerning a mature son, the believer should be in the likeness of the Heavenly Father, resembling His character and nature. In the text of *I John 3:2*, the Greek word for son is *Huios*, which means a mature son. A *Huios* or son is not gender differentiated; rather, a person can be male or female *Huios*, because the emphasis here is not gender, but God's character and nature.

> *"Now I say, That the heir, as long as he is a child, differeth nothing from a servant, though he be lord of all; But is under tutors and governors until the time appointed of the father."*
>
> *~ Galatians 4: 1-2*

In Galatians 4:1, the word *child* mentioned in the scripture refers to an immature son in his behavior. It is taken from the Greek word *Nepios* which means: immature, unlearned, simple minded son.

This must not be overlooked. Those who are given the rights to power should not function haphazardly with it but should demonstrate a certain level of maturity. It is really befitting that sons and daughters are actually mentioned in *Acts 2*. For this reason, there's a need for true Fathers in the Gospel, and some spiritual nurturing in the Body of Christ, for true affirmation. In fact, real succession has a lot to do with not only being recognized by God, but also recognized by credible leadership. This must salvage so the church can be perfected. If the next group of leaders, who are coming to the forefront, are without a sense of holiness and maturity, then the question will be, *"Is there any hope for the generation?"*

I believe there's hope!

Of a truth, spiritual leaders today must become more responsible for their sons and daughters and sons and daughters must become more accountable to their spiritual leaders. For this reason, when it comes to the Fathering spirit, there's a great need today for accountability and understanding.

Today, there are many among us who claim they have been appointed by God but have not been affirmed by anyone. Many illegitimate children have escaped the

Spiritual birthing canal and the result of this is the continuance of reproducing a culture by default and not demand. It is impossible to have true succession, when certain essentials were never passed down.

Narcissism

"Let nothing be done through strife or vainglory; but in lowliness of mind let each esteem other better than themselves. Look not every man on his own things, but every man also on the things of others." ~ Philippians 2:3-4

Narcissism is having an excessive or erotic interest in oneself rather than a having true spiritual significance or relevance.

Narcissism is a Greek term derived from the name *Narcissus*[14], who was a mythological character who fell in love with his own image. When he would not turn away from his image, he eventually died. Generally, narcissistic people are not capable of being empathetic, because their only focus is of themselves. Preserving the authenticity of the Spirit requires safeguarding the things of God.

---

[14] Mark Cartwright, "Narcissus," last modified February 20, 2017. https://www.ancient.eu/Narcissus/.

Keys to Renewal

1. Returning to the Father's Love. God is the Almighty One; He is our Abba Father, our Papa God!

   "For ye received not the spirit of bondage again unto fear; but ye received the spirit of adoption, whereby we cry, Abba, Father. The Spirit himself beareth witness with our spirit, that we are children of God"

   ~ Romans 8:15-16 ASV

2. Preserve Your Spiritual Heritage. Nothing can maintain the ongoing process of being renewed, like preserving the essential things that will maintain your spiritual heritage.

   *"And they answered Joshua, saying, All that thou commandest us we will do, and whithersoever thou sendest us, we will go. According as we hearkened unto Moses in all things, so will we hearken unto thee: only the L*ord* thy God be with thee, as he was with Moses."*

   ~ Joshua 1:16-17

3. Master Your Maturation.

Maturation is a process necessary in becoming fully developed. It is a very important requirement involved in becoming stewards of the mysteries of God.

Mysteries in Greek is the word Musterion which means hidden things that are not obvious to the natural understanding. Secret counsels that are hidden from some but revealed to others.

"And he gave some, apostles; and some, prophets; and some, evangelists; and some, pastors and teachers; For the perfecting of the saints, for the work of the ministry, for the edifying of the body of Christ: Till we all come in the unity of the faith, and of the knowledge of the Son of God, unto a perfect man, unto the measure of the stature of the fullness of Christ: That we henceforth be no more children, tossed to and fro, and carried about with every wind of doctrine, by the sleight of men, and cunning craftiness, whereby they lie in wait to deceive; But speaking the truth in love, may grow up into him in all things, which is the head, even Christ:" ~ Ephesians 4:11-15

Highlights

In Chapter Two, you have discovered the power of spiritual renewal; how it quenches the parched soul that is desperate for the fresh waters of the Spirit. Also, you have learned the importance of returning to the Father's love and how intricate it is for restoring the gift of grace in your life. In addition, this chapter discussed how the reflection of the church has become narcissistic in society today in many places. When the church no longer has a reflection of Christ, it will block the flow of God's restoring river. What was perpetuated *in Acts 2 in The* Pentecost Experience caused a succession which would place a supernatural seal upon believers for generations to come

    Furthermore, in this chapter was discussed the master key of son ship which is maturation.

Transitional Prayer

Lord, I come into your presence crying out for the refreshing springs of revival, asking you for spiritual renewal and divine restoration. Today, as I seek your face, I pray you will eradicate anything in me that would hinder your hand upon my life. I pray for maturation to take place in my life and that you would give me strength to submit to the process that is designed to develop me into one of your mature children. Lord, I ask you to cause Christ to be formed in me. I yield to your Holy Spirit help me to keep my eyes on you.
In the name of Jesus Christ. Amen!

Chapter Three
Cultural Assimilation

Follow my example, as I follow the example of Christ. I praise you for remembering me in everything and for holding to the traditions just as I passed them on to you.
~ I Corinthians 11:1-2

Though certain traditions of the early church have drastically changed from their originality, some are vital in preserving its true heritage and culture. Ideologies and perspectives have formed various groups and certain religious preferences, which have made up many different church cultures within our society at large. Cultures are derived from values, and mindsets, which foster systems of beliefs and patterns that create an ethos. An Ethos is the characteristic spirit of an era, or community that creates a culture. Every church's culture functions like a human ethos, it reveals how and what certain groups do and why they do, what they do.

Cultural assimilation is the process of reproducing culture by assimilating it. Cultural assimilation in the church is when the Church reproduces its own community and culture. This can be good and bad. When people are authentically regenerated in God's Kingdom, they will produce cultures that are an accurate description, of what they are supposed to be and function in the earth. However, when unprofitable cycles are consistently being produced, people and movements are artificially assimilated.

A blood culture[15] is a test taken by medical personnel to detect the blood of foreign invasion such as, bacteria and other microorganisms. When a person is sick, a blood culture is taken to detect any infection or decrease in their bloodstream. Just as a blood culture will medically determine how healthy a person's body is, the church's culture works the same way. It will reveal the condition of that body of believers. The healthier a person's church culture is, the more they have a chance of being spiritually healthy. One way or another, cultures will reproduce themselves.

Church Cultures

The greatest need in Christendom today is to establish a healthy spiritual environment, which produces cultures that personify true convictions for Christ.

Across the planet today, there is an evolving seeker-sensitive generation[16]. When it comes to their church culture's preferences, they have more of a -*please don't offend me*- attitude. "Just let me be entertained".

Props and practicality are becoming a desired trend. Sadly, many churches are even losing their zeal for prayer and the great commission.

---

15 Brian Kran and Brian Wu, "Blood Culture" last modified January 4, 2017. https://www.healthline.com/health/blood-culture#overview1.

16 T.C. McMahon, "The Seeker-Friendly Way of Doing Church". March 2004. https://www.thebereancall.org.

The seeker-sensitive church culture thrives to be trendy and relevant with the times. Basically, their paradigm is, *"How much of the world can we get away with to lure the people to us?"* There is something wrong with this paradigm, it is certainly faulty. When people do not realize that people are coming to the church because they urgently need God and are longing to have an experience with Him that would literally change their lives forever, they will miss the opportunity to serve them. Even worse, when desperate souls look for transformation by going to church, the seeker sensitive paradigm can only offer them entertainment and some practical humor in return. It is a great travesty when believers forget that their hearts were also void, until God filled it with Himself.

Unfortunately, many today have conformed to this ideology. You will know a seeker-sensitive church because it is hard to spiritually express yourself there. You can't be too loud, and there's not a lot of radical worship in the service. Speaking in tongues is definitely a *no, no!* The people who attend these types of churches would probably say, all of these things are not necessary and are only emotionalism. This is also wrong thinking because true worship comes from having deep intimacy with God. In pursuit of the presence of God, may we regain the key of David.

"Enter into his gates with thanksgiving, and into his courts with praise: be thankful unto him and bless his name. For the LORD is good; his mercy is everlasting; and his truth endureth to all generations."

~ Psalm 100:4-5

When David became king, he laid out the schoolmaster for obtaining the presence and glory of God. He drew the dividing line between true worship verse casual practicalities.

Intimate worship is vitally important to manifest the presence of God. Generally, a church's worship style will give the distinction of its culture.

Now the attempt here is not to condemn or badger anyone's church, but to let the truth be known. There are many things that are being embraced today that voids true authenticity. For instance, although seeker-sensitive churches are not as spiritually advanced, some of the traditionally inherited behavioral patterns have not fostered true reformation. This can occur when God is not the real focus of one's affection.

Furthermore, just because a person speaks in tongues, jump, dance, and roll around on the floor, does not exempt them from missing the mark!

Good theatrics can easily give the appearance of a true experience with the Almighty. When one has a certain level of charisma but is not willing to be reformed by the Spirit, then that person's paradigm is no greater than the seeker-sensitive paradigm. Generally, people who are like this are sensationalism seekers. Sensationalism does not require you to ascribe to the Almighty. For instance, you can have all the hoopla and pageantry you want, but if you do not possess real intimacy with God, you will not have the power of God.

> *Sensationalism:*
> 1. The doctrine of judging by the gratification of the senses.
>
> 2. The doctrine that all ideas are derived from and are essentially reducible to sensations.

"For I bear them record that they have a zeal of God, but not according to knowledge. For they being ignorant of God's righteousness, and going about to establish their own righteousness, have not submitted themselves unto the righteousness of God." ~ Romans 10:2-3

Having zeal for God is not a bad thing. In fact, it is good to have it. Zeal keeps you motivated and excited about what God is doing. However, be not mistaken, having zeal without substance and knowledge is unfruitful.

Some people get comfortable with just having a good time in church and end up only with zeal, failing to understand, that the greatest part of a God experience is the transformation of one's life, which impacts others. Whenever you allow church to become escapism from the world around you, you will become a prisoner of religion!

The Big Bang Theory

The Big Bang Theory: a concept in which people have built their entire ministries on. As the Body of Believers, we must be leery of this.

In Christendom, in our modern society, there is a misconception among those who believe that unless you are living in lap of luxury and are appealing to multiplied thousands, you are insignificant. This mindset is the furthest thing from the truth! Church growth should never be determined by quantity alone, but by the vessels that are being developed and poured into, who will impact the world around them.

"And the word of God increased; and the number of the disciples multiplied in Jerusalem greatly; and a great company of the priests were obedient to the faith." ~ Acts 6:7

The real example of church growth is in Acts, chapter six. The scripture gives the pictorial of growth governed by the prioritizing of prayer, God's word and evangelism.

Every pastor's dream is to see their membership multiply, which is a good thing. However, membership should never have preference over the pursuit of salvation.

In *Acts 2:47*, the Bible says, *"the Lord added to the church daily such as should be saved."* By the time you get to *Acts 6*, the numbers of members were not just being added, but the numbers of believers multiplied.

In Acts 6, the church had experienced exponential growth. The leaders committed their lives to praying and fasting. This exposes the fact that when a church focus and main priority is prayer, fasting, salvation, and yielding to the Holy Spirit, it will eventually experience organic growth.

How true that increase can be a great indication of God doing phenomenal things. Exponential growth can be a great sign of true productivity and the spirit of faith. However, growth is not always determined in numbers. Growth can be determined by discipleship and people getting equipped to impact and invade their spheres for the Kingdom of God.

Unfortunately, when a church holds several services on Sunday Mornings, all flowing in the same manner, word for word, and given a specific time frame, then it is longer a setting for God to move, but a program. This can easily resemble *Show Business*.

Lights, Cameras, Action!!!!

It is good when grace has been extended for exponential growth. But let's not negate the fact that, just because something is big, does not mean it has the substance God wants it to have. On the other hand, just because something appears small in stature, does not mean it is not great in value or have phenomenal potential. Grander-ism and drawing big crowds do not always mean that people have a sincere appetite for the things of God.

By all means, I am not saying that it is not a great thing to experience great growth, because it is! But I have news for you....

"Small is the New Big!!!!"

The Power of Small Things

"A little one shall become a thousand, and a small one a strong nation: I the LORD will hasten it in his time." ~ Isaiah 60:22

Did you know that a proton is one of the smallest particles in the universe? It is smaller than an atom and cannot be seen with the naked eye. When one compares an atom to a proton, the atom would be the size of a football field and the proton would be smaller than a marble.

Although, the proton is tiny in size, it is essentially needed to make up the nucleus of an atom[17].

> *"He told them another parable: "The kingdom of heaven is like a mustard seed, which a man took and planted in his field. Though it is the smallest of all seeds, yet when it grows, it is the largest of garden plants and becomes a tree, so that the birds come and perch in its branches."*
>
> *~ Matthew 13:31-32*

    In the scriptures, Jesus discusses about the mustard seed and how it is smaller than all the other seeds. Fortunately, when it reaches its full potential, it is large enough for birds to build their nest in its branches. The principle behind this parable is one must never mistake the power of small things. Just because a thing is small in size, does not mean it is not great in power! In fact, God is strategically rising up smaller hubs across the country today with the sole purpose of developing teams with a global cause to impact nations. Gospel celebrities whose only focus is drawing large crowds are gradually fading away, while smaller gatherings are rising with a greater perspective for God's Glory and Kingdom.

---

[17] Karen Carr, "What Is A Proton? Atom and Chemistry" last modified June 2, 2017. http://quatr.us/chemistry/atoms/proton.htm.

As the church moves into the 21st century, great peril has invaded the Earth. There is a *"No More Church as Usual"* attitude that is sweeping the nation among God chasers. While many see church today as a waste of time, and energy; healthy churches are fundamental in the transformation of its members' lives.

The Healthy Church

"And they continued steadfastly in the apostles' doctrine and fellowship, and in breaking of bread, and in prayers. And fear came upon every soul: and many wonders and signs were done by the apostles. And all that believed were together, and had all things common;" ~Acts 2:42-44

Every church has its own spiritual culture. Therefore, every church is not for everyone. For this reason, whatever church a person is appointed to, they are there so it can help fulfill their spiritual needs and calling.

Acts 2:42, reveals a healthy church culture. Here are some quality attributes the early church exhibited to establish a healthy culture:

1. The early church was birthed out of prayer.

2. They remained in the Apostles' Doctrine, and by Gods, word they governed their lives.

3. They fellowshipped with one another and had all things in common. (They were unified)

4. Miracles broke out among them which was an indication God had full preeminence; He was not contained in a religious box.

5. They were skillful in the market place. They had effective strategies for commerce.

6. The early church kept the faith and God continually grew the church. The characteristics of a healthy spiritual culture must be consistently developed, and God will grow the church.

These qualities are for healthy spiritual growth.

"But the hour cometh, and now is, when the true worshippers shall worship the Father in spirit and in truth: for the Father seeketh such to worship him." ~ John 4:23

Religious settings with repeated, powerless practices will resist a real worship experience; these environments normally suffer from spiritual deprivation.

Generally, people who attend churches with fresh worship service, and preach and teach applicable biblical principles, are people who are spiritually nourished and receive clear directives from Heaven. Here is something I believe is of great importance, any religious practice that is done the same way over and over again, will become boring and ineffective! When you allow the Holy Spirit to do as He will, you will open yourself up to new adventures and new spiritual terrains.

"Remember ye not the former things, neither consider the things of old. Behold, I will do a new thing; now it shall spring forth; shall ye not know it? I will even make a way in the wilderness, and rivers in the desert." ~ Isaiah 43:18-19

The river of the Spirit will come with fresh outpourings and will not flow from dried up brooks of yesterday but will come with refreshing springs that are new every morning.

Keys to Renewal

When you progressively pursue the Holy Spirit, He will break the constraints that keep you where He was yesterday and will propel you into where He is in the now.

Whatever hinders transition hinders transformation and becomes an impediment to spiritual renewal.

"And no man putteth new wine into old bottles: else the new wine doth burst the bottles, and the wine is spilled, and the bottles will be marred: but new wine must be put into new bottles." ~ Mark 2:22

Highlights

In Chapter Three, various paradigms were discovered that were not essential to keeping the authenticity of the things of God, while other essentials were advantageous. Warnings of the pitfalls of cultural assimilation were also discussed throughout this chapter.

Transitional Prayer

Holy Spirit draw me near you, transform and renew my mind. Breathe in me new life and cause me to know you. This one thing I desire, to dwell in your presence fascinated by your beauty and ever learning at your feet. Your mercies are new every morning. Great is your faithfulness towards me. Free me from the strongholds of religion. Let the fresh outpouring of your presence transcend me. I give you my heart and fix my eyes on you. Continue your process of ever-changing me and cause me to forever know your ways.
   In Jesus' name. Amen!

Chapter Four
The Synergistic Spiritual Development

"And he took the mantle of Elijah that fell from him, and smote the waters, and said, Where is the LORD God of Elijah? and when he also had smitten the waters, they parted hither and thither: and Elisha went over." ~ 2Kings 2:14

Synergy is the interaction of more than one agent or entities to produce a combined effect greater than the sum of its separate effects. The term synergy come from the Greek words, *synergia* and *synergos*, which means *working together*.

Impartation and activation are the two major forces involved in the synergistic of spiritual development. These two forces are laws to spiritual growth that will determine succession. Impartation and activation are very powerful and dually rewarding. Also, they are a major force in discipleship. Today, many people are spiritually deficient, because they never received proper fathering, mentoring or were never poured into.

Naturally, fathers are nurturers and protectors. The role of spiritual fathers is to do the same thing. Spiritual fathers raise their spiritual children to be spiritually healthy. Spiritual fathers give affirmation, wisdom, counsel, direction, and correction. A sure mark of a great destiny is the impartation or handprint of a father who have set the sails for His children's success.

Spiritual fathers are also mentors. A mentor is

someone who trains, imparts, and disciples a mentee. A mentee learns from and is imparted into from their mentor. The relationship of a mentor and a mentee is like a teacher, student relationship. Unfortunately, there are people who hold offices and titles today who have never been a student. Now, that may look one way in the church, but I'm sure there's a total greater concern that one might have in the hospital or court room. I'm sure your concern would be that your Dr. has a PhD or that your lawyer practiced law at an accredited University.
Well it's the same principle for those who are in the business of souls...

A disciple is an advert learner; one who submits himself or herself under a teacher. A true disciple receives an impartation of the grace gift, which is on their mentor's or leader's life and will be activated to do great works.

However, as long as a person is not submitted to a spiritual authority, they will never partake in a great anointing. This type of renegade behavior has a very dangerous consequence. For instance, a spiritual father, mentor, or someone who is in spiritual authority can detect when you are in error. Unfortunately, when a person is not accountable to spiritual authority, they will easily fall into the trap of deception.

Nowadays, when people, who have not been submitted to spiritual authority, attempts to go into the ministry, they usually will be zealous but will lack a great deal of temperance. On the other hand, when a person has submitted themselves to spiritual authority and has received a credible impartation they will go forth in the power of

The power of Spirit! In 2Kings, Chapter 2, Elisha experienced this after receiving a double portion of the gracing that was on his spiritual father's, Elijah, life.

Becoming a disciple is key to effectively carrying out your divine assignment. It is impossible to operate in the supernatural when you have not been activated.

"That is why I remind you to fan into flame the gracious gift of God, [that inner fire—the special endowment] which is in you through the laying on of my hands [with those of the elders at your ordination]." ~ 2 Timothy 1:6 (AMP)

Apostle Paul is speaking into the life of his spiritual son, Timothy. He informed him of what was imparted to him. Paul told his spiritual son that he received this impartation through the laying on of hands. Also, he encouraged Timothy to fan the flame. This verse is the sole purpose of an impartation. To be activated to go forth and do the works of God.

Impartations are not only received through the laying on of hands, but also through spiritual transferences. Spiritual transferences occur through teachings, preaching, and serving. In addition, the characteristics of a spiritual authority can be transferred to a mentee or spiritual son or daughter who is consistently in their presence.

Biblical Examples of Synergistic Spiritual Development

"And Joshua the son of Nun was full of the spirit of wisdom; for Moses had laid his hands upon him: and the children of Israel hearkened unto him, and did as the L<small>ORD</small> commanded Moses."

~ Deuteronomy 34:9

In examining Joshua's succession in leadership, you will find that his success was not of own merits, but first and foremost he was Gods next choice after Moses and because he was receptive to Mosses' leadership. This is a true statement; good followers can be developed into great leaders, but those who refuse to be led will struggle with leading others. Joshua followed Moses' leadership so well until he perfected it and it prepared him for leadership. When God commissioned Joshua, He commanded Moses to lay hands on him to receive an impartation from him. This was not the only time those of Moses' leadership received an impartation from him. Seventy of his elders also received an impartation from the laying on of his hands.

Even Jesus received an impartation at two important places in his life. The Jordan River and the wilderness of temptation were two defining moments of His ministry.

> *"And Jesus, when he was baptized, went up straightway out of the water: and, lo, the heavens were opened unto him, and he saw the Spirit of God descending like a dove, and lighting upon him: And lo a voice from heaven, saying, This is my beloved Son, in whom I am well pleased." ~ Matthew 3:16-17*

John the Baptist was a forerunner of Jesus Christ. His ministry in the wilderness was to prepare the way of the son of the living God. John's part was very intricate in imparting into the life of Jesus. By baptizing Jesus, John prophetically transferred the priesthood from the Levitical order to the order of Melchizedek. This was a crucial prophetic act. Jesus would become the new high priest of a new and living way.

After Jesus was submerged in the Jordan River; the Holy Spirit descended upon Him and His Father in Heaven affirmed Him. This let us know true affirmation precedes activation.

In Matthew 4:1, after baptism, Jesus was led in the wilderness. For forty days, he was tempted of the devil. When Jesus came out of the wilderness of temptation, He was fully activated for ministry.

There is something very important that you must pay close attention to here. His ministry did not officially start until He received John the Baptist's impartation at the

Jordan River. After Jesus came out of the wilderness of testing He was activated to do the work of ministry. After a person receives an impartation, activation will follow. In the principle of first things first; certain things must go first, and lead out. When people refuse this prophetic principle, they become like blind guides.

The Power Twins

Impartation and activation both can be looked upon as the power twins. They both are highly transferable. The difference in the two is, one can receive an impartation through the laying of hands, teaching and environments that are spiritually contagious. On the other hand, activation is the active force of an impartation, which causes demonstration and manifestation. Whenever a person receives an impartation, activation will proceed. An *authentic impartation releases the activating force for exploits.*

Great exploits will come with great momentum. Momentum is the driving force that causes impact. When people have been properly activated, they should experience not only movement but momentum as well. Unfortunately, sometimes you will find more movement and emotional hype than momentum. This means for some people their God-Experience has become like an amusement park. For example, there's a lot of movement on a roller coaster, but when you get off of it, you are dizzy and excited but have not gone anywhere! For some people it is just like that; full of excitement, but void of momentum.

An amusement park can have a great deal of excitement and fantasy, but you cannot stay there all day. When the park closes you will get back in your automobile, go back home and all you are left with are memories. The moment of escapism is over! Unfortunately, some of our religious experiences are just like the amusement park. People get amused, but never get activated, or learn to sustain the experience.

In *Matthew 10:1*, Jesus released His impartation to the twelve disciples. The Bible records, *He called them unto Himself and gave them power against unclean spirits to cast them out and to heal all manner of sickness and diseases.* Also, in *Matthew 10:7-8*, Jesus sent them forth to proclaim the Kingdom of Heaven was at hand, to heal the sick, clean the leprosy, raise the dead, and cast out devils.

Jesus said to them, *freely they received and freely they gave.*

What did they receive?

They received an impartation from Jesus and were activated to go forth and share it with others. Because of His impartation, His disciples experienced something extraordinary. They received an Impartation to engage in the Supernatural.

They entered a Dimension of Power with Him! The great

Mystery behind this was that they were privileged to experience the power of the Holy Spirit, before the initial outpouring of it at Pentecost.

This was not religious or emotional hype, but a true impartation of His power. The Greek word for power is *Dunamis* which is explosive power and ability. *The Kingdom of God is not a matter of talk, but power! (1 Corinthians 4:20).* It is only when a believer receives the impartation of the Holy Spirit will they become proficient in the things of the God.

Here are more scriptural accounts of impartation and activation.

"And the LORD came down in a cloud, and spake unto him, and took of the spirit that was upon him, and gave it unto the seventy elders: and it came to pass, that, when the spirit rested upon them, they prophesied, and did not cease." ~ Numbers 11:25

"And he laid his hands upon him, and gave him a charge, as the LORD commanded by the hand of Moses." ~ Numbers 27:23

"Then Samuel took the horn of oil, and anointed him in the midst of his brethren: and the Spirit of the LORD came upon David from that day forward. So, Samuel rose up and went to Ramah."

~ I Samuel 16:13

And Joshua the son of Nun was full of the spirit of wisdom; for Moses had laid his hands upon him: and the children of Israel hearkened unto him and did as the LORD commanded Moses.

~ Deuteronomy 34:9

Whom they set before the apostles: and when they had prayed, they laid their hands on them.

~Acts 6:6

Principles of Receiving Impartation and Activation

Principle 1: *You must be a willing and attentive learner.*

"The things [the doctrine, the precepts, the admonitions, the sum of my ministry] which you have heard me teach in the presence of many witnesses, entrust [as a treasure] to reliable and faithful men who will also be capable and qualified to teach others."

-2 Timothy 2:2 (AMP)

Principle 2: *Put into practice what has been imparted to you.*

"Whatever you have learned or received or heard from me or seen in me put it into practice. And the God of peace will be with you." - Philippians 4:9

Principle 3: *Use discernment when determining your teachers. Wisdom is imparted in the company of the prudent, but deficiency is the pathway of the unlearned.*

"He that walketh with wise men shall be wise: but a companion of fools shall be destroyed." -Proverbs 13:20

Principle 4: *The steps of a successful person, will eventually lead to success.*

"Mark the blameless man [who is spiritually complete], and behold the upright [who walks in moral integrity]; There is a [good] future for the man of peace [because a life of honor blesses one's descendants]."   *-Psalms 37:37 (AMP)*

Principle 5: *What is transferable is sometimes irrevocable.*

"Lay hands suddenly on no man, neither be partaker of other men's sins: keep thyself pure."   *-I Timothy 5:22*

"And Jacob went near unto Isaac his father; and he felt him, and said, The voice is Jacob's voice, but the hands are the hands of Esau. And he discerned him not, because his hands were hairy, as his brother Esau's hands: so, he blessed him."

-Genesis 27:22-23

Keys to Renewal

Having the willingness to learn will determine what you're able to communicate and impart to others. The virtue of things imparted, lives in those who position themselves to receive. Being attentive to the wisdom of the wise will eventually make one wiser.

Highlights

In Chapter Four, you were enlightened about the synergistic of spiritual development. You found out about two important components that are synergistically rewarding, impartation and activation. These components act as power twins that are vital in discipleship and will equip you for good success.

Transitional Prayer

Father, I thank you for the purpose you have given me. Thank you for those who you have placed in my life to help develop and cultivate my character. Let me identify with the spiritual leaders who watch over my soul. Lord I eagerly receive the wisdom that comes through them, that is from you. Help me to remain humble and not get puffed up, assuming that I don't need anyone. Lord teach me, to humble myself under your mighty hand and wait patiently on your timing to lift me higher. Holy Spirit you are the imparter who imparts gifts unto men and uses them to impart into others.

Make me a yielded vessel that I may receive the active force of your power, to go forth and experience the wonders and exploits of your kingdom.

In the name of your dear son Jesus Christ.
Amen!

Chapter Five
Spirit of Reformation

"Repent ye therefore, and be converted, that your sins may be blotted out, when the times of refreshing shall come from the presence of the Lord. And he shall send Jesus Christ, which before was preached unto you: Whom the heaven must receive until the times of restitution of all things, which God hath spoken by the mouth of all his holy prophets since the world began."

~ Acts 3:19-21

Whenever a time of refreshing comes, it will be proceeded by the winds of reformation and spiritual renewal. Although there is much indifference within Christian society, yet the quest for restitution and reformation will always find a way to arise. Though the pursuits for it today are subtle, reformation can be traced all the way back to the 1300s, when the Pope's governing seat was moved from Rome to France[18] and brought great controversy. Just as in any era, whenever character and moral values are

---

[18] "Avignon Papacy," *Encyclopedia Britannica*, last modified December 31, 2014, https://www.britannica.com/event/Avignon-papacy.

tested, reformers will rise up as change agents to bring things back into alignment.

> **"Do not move the ancient landmark [at the boundary of the property] Which your fathers have set."** ~ ***Proverbs 22:28 AMP***

In the early 1500s, a young Augustinian monk by the name of Martin Luther challenged the Roman Catholic Church in such a way that it gave birth to a new reformation called Protestantism. Luther and his supporters were against what they depicted as errors in the Roman Catholic Church. The movement began in 1517 after Luther had published a thesis he had written against the abuse in the sale of indulgence. Although there were attempts by other reformers at that time to reform the Roman Catholic Church, only Luther succeeded in sparking the movement.

Luther was ridiculed for his stand and desire to reform beliefs. Once while being challenged, he openly stated that he could not deny the truth of God's Word, because his conscience was captive to it. This statement alone reveals that one's conscience is the light that exposes the level of truth they have really embraced. It gives proof of the authenticity of one's personal reformation.

In his times, Martin Luther's appeal was to the soul and conscience of humanity. He aimed to steer the hearts of his peers back to biblical landmarks, which, eventually, shook the Catholic Movement.

Luther's reformation swept throughout Europe in the sixteenth century. The reformation followed centuries of theological debates which addressed the religious and moral diminution in the Western Church.

By all means, the Protestant Movement did not embrace all of the original essentials of the New Testament Church. However, it was the bridge and catalyst that brought forth many changes to come. In fact, the charismatic movement of our day stemmed from it, and now there is an emerging of both Protestant and Catholic Charismatics[19].

Martin Luther was a great reformer. Along with other reformers before him, he released the spirit of reformation to his generation. What must be echoed from this is, whenever the spirit of reformation comes, it will always present truth with the intent of causing a paradigm shift that will foster a movement of change. After the reformation era of Martin Luther, great revivalists such as James McGready, George Whitefield, Asahel Nettleton, and Charles Finney also emerged during those times.

---

[19] "Martin Luther," *A & E Television Networks*, last modified August 8, 2017, https://www.biography.com.

Every reformer, who carries the spirit of reformation, releases restoration to a generation.

As a whole, the Spirit Reformation comes, to restore lost and abandoned essentials that were given to the Church God's governing Body.

"And he gave some, apostles; and some, prophets; and some, evangelists; and some, pastors and teachers; For the perfecting of the saints, for the work of the ministry, for the edifying of the body of Christ:" ~ Ephesians 4:11-12

In the last decade, there has been a restoration of the fivefold ministry which has caused an emergence of apostles and prophets in the Body of Christ.

Despite the errors of our era, God's Body is being realigned to fulfill the great commission. The great commission is more than what we do in our church buildings alone. More importantly, the great commission is what we do outside the four walls of the church to impact the society around us.

The kingdoms of this world were lost in the fall of man in the Garden of Eden, but through Christ's atoning sacrifice at the cross; glory, power, and dominion has been restored to the church. As a result of this, the essential truth that brings the power of the gospel must be restored through the freshness of the Holy Spirit.

Mundane religious practices are sterile and obsolete, and only make Christ's atoning sacrifice null and void. This is what hinders people from experiencing God's power.

Fortunately, reformations cause change and things to be brought back into order. On the other hand, religious doctrinal systems do not predicate or promote change, only ineffective traditions. Reformation affects religious, social, political, and economic systems in order to bring improvement and proper alignments. Also, the spirit of reformation brings clarity of truth. In these end times, God will raise up a generation of modern day reformers that will be ordinary people, who have been transformed by the Spirit of truth, and will impact the world for the Kingdom of God.

Overall, whenever reformation comes, there will always be a time of refreshing that will precede it. Reformations will come and the latter and former rain will simultaneously shower the Earth, with the refreshing presence of the living God.

Reformation Restores Foundational things...

"If the foundations [of a godly society] are destroyed, What can the righteous do?"

~ Psalm 11:3 AMP

"And God hath set some in the church, first apostles, secondarily prophets, thirdly teachers, after that miracles, then gifts of healings, helps, governments, diversities of tongues."

~ I Corinthians 12:28

When the foundational things that are originally designed to uphold a structure are removed, then there are no grounds for it to stand on. A foundation will keep things securely in place. In functionality, the church of the Lord Jesus Christ started out apostolic, and it will go out the same way.

According to Acts 3:21, what has been happening from the start and through the finish of the Church is the restoration of all things. It is the spirit of reformation that is causing this to happen. Every time an old reformation concludes, a new reformation comes to replace it. That is why some Christians are stagnated today. Old reformations that have ceased from spiritually growing, are no longer able to transition people into the next level of their spiritual journey. For this reason, new reformations should not be about doctrinal differences, but fresh revelation from the Holy Spirit.

Reformation Brings Recovery

"So, he went with them. And when they came to Jordan, they cut down wood. But as one was felling a beam, the axe head fell into the water: and he cried, and said, Alas, master! for it was borrowed.

And the man of God said, Where fell it? And he shewed him the place. And he cut down a stick and cast it in thither; and the iron did swim."

~ 2Kings 6:4-6

The story of the lost axe head is a story of recovery. It is about recovering something essential that was lost. The axe was an effective tool for working and without the axe head it was no good to the young man who borrowed it, or its owner. Once the axe head was recovered, with joy this young man was able to effectively complete his assignment and return the tool back to its rightful owner. Reformation is the same way. It happens for the sole purpose of Kingdom recovery.

When the initial outpouring of the Holy Spirit came, it came with the spirit of reformation and revival. Since that time, there have been seasons of renewal and times of refreshing where the Holy Spirit has been poured upon generations. In fact, we are coming into the timing, of a reformation that the Body of Christ has never seen before that will bring fresh winds of revival across the land.

Keys to Renewal

Whenever the spirit of reformation comes, it will present restored truth, that will cause new paradigms and progressive changes.

Highlights

Chapters Five informatively took us on a journey of the past and present to discover how reformers emerged through time and restored original essentials of truth, thereby fostering a spirit of reformation onto their generation. We found out that true reformation, brings change that is often ignited by reformers, who God raises up and empowers to provoke change.

Transitional Prayer

Father, thank you for sending your Spirit of Reformation to this generation. Your word declares, that you would raise up a generation that would seek after you and that you would restore the things that have been lost. Let reformation begin in me. Cause your light to break out like the dawn and your life to quickly spring forth in me. Let your righteousness go before me, leading me into peace and your glory as my rear guard.

In the name of Jesus I make this declaration. Amen and amen!

Chapter Six
A Paradigm Shift

"Now therefore ye are no more strangers and foreigners, but fellow citizens with the saints and of the household of God; And are built upon the foundation of the apostles and prophets, Jesus Christ himself being the chief corner stone;"

~ Ephesians 2:19-20

In the latter 21st century, a sovereign awakening has begun to take place. People are starting to leave the net of religiosity and are starting to embrace the Newness of what God is doing.

Although there is great religious variety today, there is yet an enlightening transition that has taken off across the planet. People are beginning to have a deeper hunger for God. Former landmarks are starting to be abandoned and new paradigms are being embraced.

In the beginning of the millennium, there came a resurgence of the fivefold ministry. Apostles and prophets were restored to their functionality in the Body of Christ. This great restoration propagated a new reformation among believers.

There were certain end time reformers like Bishop Bill Hammond who had formally prophetically declared that in the coming moves of God there would be an emergence of modern day apostles and prophets. The new millennium would be the beginning of the second apostolic and prophetic age.

Though some Christians have accepted this paradigm shift, some still struggle with the idea of modern day apostles and prophets – even though, after His resurrection, Jesus Christ instituted the entire fivefold, as ascension gifts to the Body of Christ. Unfortunately, today, many have relegated the movement to mere super phraseology.

For this reason, many want to know really, *"What is the Apostolic and Prophetic?"* Well, first let's talk about what it is not as opposed to what it is. This is a reformation that is not based on catechisms, robes and vestments, or doctrines that pertain to religious rules and regulations that keep people shackled in legalism. And it is not geared around only these two offices, but aims for the restoration of all five gifts, to perfect the church and perpetuate the kingdom of God. The apostolic and prophetic is a movement of the saints. It is overall the continuance of Jesus' ministry through the lives of believers. It is the ministry that was delivered from Jesus to His apostles and the saints, who are His apostolic people on the Earth.

> ***"Wherefore, holy brethren, partakers of the heavenly calling, consider the Apostle and High Priest of our profession, Christ Jesus;"***
>
> ***~ Hebrews 3:1***

The word Apostolic comes from the root word Apostle, which is a fivefold ascension gift. The office of the apostles is one of the fivefold ministry gifts. However, the Apostolic Spirit is meant to rest upon all born again, Spirit filled believers.

The noun *Apostolos* is derived from the verb *Apostello*, which means sent or commissioned. The apostolic itself is an equipping and sending dimension of the fivefold ministry. Apostolic leaders focus on the spiritual development of believers, so they can be effective in and outside of the church. *Most importantly, the Apostolic Spirit advances the Kingdom of God!*

12 Earmarks of an Apostolic Culture

1. Developers of Disciples
2. Fervent in Prayer
3. Intense Worshipers
4. Prophetic in Nature
5. Great Appreciation for the Gifts of the Spirit
6. Strong in Deliverance
7. Embraces the Fivefold Ministry
8. Stewards of God's Presence

9. Revelatory Teaching and Preaching

10. Manifestation of God's Kingdom

11. Zeal for the Great Commission

12. Marketplace Mentality

Apostolic Synchronization

"And the LORD went before them by day in a pillar of a cloud, to lead them the way; and by night in a pillar of fire, to give them light; to go by day and night:" ~ Exodus 13:21

Synchronicity:

1. To cause to indicate the same time, as one timepiece with another, to cause to occur or operate at the same exact time or rate.

2. To cause to move, operate; work, etc., at the same rate and exactly together: in harmony or harmonious relationship.

3. To cause (sound and action) to match precisely: to synchronize the sound of footsteps with another's movements, or to match the sound and actions.

4. To cause to agree in time of occurrence; assign to the same time or period.

In the wilderness, Israel's success was determined by how well they were synchronized with God's timing. Their ability to move together, following the cloud by day and the pillar of fire by night caused them to experience God's providence.

"And now I am no more in the world, but these are in the world, and I come to thee. Holy Father, keep through thine own name those whom thou hast given me, that they may be one, as we are."

~ John 17:11

Everything in life has a rhythm!

In apostolic synchronization, believers are unified and flow in the rhythm of the Spirit. The Holy Spirit's objective is to have an intimate relationship with us. We are becoming one with Him. Originally, America has been a major forerunner of Christianity to the world, but when the gates of the church are open to separatism, then division hinders us from marching to the syncopation of the Holy Spirit.

"until we all reach oneness in the faith and in the knowledge of the Son of God, [growing spiritually] to become a mature believer, reaching to the measure of the fullness of Christ [manifesting His spiritual completeness and exercising our spiritual gifts in unity]." ~ Ephesians 4:13 AMP

When the Body of Christ is truly in synch together, we will begin to be productive and proactive and will fulfill our purpose here on Earth. Often, what breaks spiritual productivity is a disenfranchised spirit. When God's Kingdom is disenfranchised, it cannot meet the urgent need of demand and supply. When believers flow together, they will develop a Christ-centered culture that will build communities and influence the masses. This exposes the pink elephant in the room that must be addressed.

"You can't have apostolic synchronization if there is racial bias!

Just like in the early revivals in the 1900s, a real move of God will break the spirit of indifference and will release the flow of healing and restoration. I really believe that every church should have a multicultural vision or at least welcome all people regardless of their ethnic backgrounds.

Regardless of status, socio-background or race, the universal depiction of Heaven includes all ethnicities. The church should be a type and shadow of what Heaven looks like. Status quo and stereotypes do not have a place in the Body of Christ. Thus unification can never be accomplished if we are not synchronized together as one people and army of the living God.

> *"Even them will I bring to my holy mountain and make them joyful in my house of prayer: their burnt offerings and their sacrifices shall be accepted upon mine altar; for mine house shall be called a house of prayer for all people."*
>
> *~ Isaiah 56:7*

God is the desire of all nations. He desires to raise a people who would influence cities and transform cultures within them. Our actual assignment is to become Kingdom Ambassadors, who will influence the kingdoms of this world. In apostolic synchronization, the Body of Christ must unify in order to impact the world around us.

> *"And Jesus knew their thoughts, and said unto them, Every kingdom divided against itself is brought to desolation; and every city or house divided against itself shall not stand:"*
>
> *~ Matthew 12:25*

Keys to Renewal

"And [His gifts to the church were varied and] He Himself appointed some as apostles [special messengers, representatives], some as prophets [who speak a new message from God to the people], some as evangelists [who spread the good news of salvation], and some as pastors and teachers [to shepherd and guide and instruct]"

~ Ephesians 4:11 AMP

The succession of any authentic move of God depends on the unification of the contenders of it. God's undeserved favor has not been given indiscriminately, but in manifold ways to first restore the leadership of the church, then unify the Body of Christ, so that the world can come to know Jesus Christ as Lord and savior.

Highlights

In Chapter Six, we discovered the missing link; the fivefold ministry. In Ephesians 4, all of the ascension gifts were instituted by Jesus Christ to equip and perfect the body of believers, the church of the living God, and to do the work of the ministry. Also, we were enlightened on the importance of apostolic synchronicity and how imperative it is for believers in Christ to be united together in the unity of the faith and the detriment of being divided.

Transitional Prayer

Lord I come into your presence, asking that you would purge my heart and pour out your Spirit upon me. Break off the shackles of prejudice and indifference. Set me free from any racial divide. Synchronize me with your Holy Spirit and your body the church. Just as Jesus and you are one, make us one and complete in you; Until we all reach oneness in the faith and the knowledge of the Son of God, growing spiritually to become mature believers, reaching the measure of the fullness of Christ, manifesting His spiritual completeness, exercising our spiritual gifts in love and unity. Let the world see you in us and bring glory to your name!

In the name of your dear son Jesus Christ! Amen!

Chapter Seven
Glory Global

"For the earth shall be filled with the knowledge of the glory of the LORD***, as the waters cover the sea."***
~ Habakkuk 2:14

In order for the Earth to be filled with the knowledge of God, the church must come out of dormancy and become the manifestation of God's will on the Earth! This is accomplished through the act of mobilization.

Mobilization is a military term that means to marshal military into readiness for active service. During World War I, military mobilization became a defining aspect of American history. Previously, America had no preparation for war and its need for mobilization became imperative. Being that the decision to enter World War I was made; the country was now tasked with having to hastily prepare for battle. Troops needed to be established which introduced the drafting process in an effort to increase the United States Army and several federal agencies were formed to create and regulate funding for war[20]. Through this initial act of Mobilization, the presence of the American Army strengthened. Although it has significantly changed since then, the strategic involvement is still highly effective from its birthing in 1917, yet it allowed it to become what it is today.

---

[20] "WWI Mobilization," Siteseen, accessed August 19, 2017. http://www.american-historama.org.

The concept of mobilization should also be considered in advancing God's Kingdom. The church is God's triumphant army that He is raising up to impact and influence the entire globe for His Kingdom. However, the opposite of mobilization is demobilization, which is to disband. To demobilize is to become stagnant and to have no means of protection or defense. The effect-ability of the 21st century church highly depends on its mobilization.

Through the concept of mobilization, the internet, media, marketplace, and various fields of occupation have now become major fields of evangelism, which is presenting to today's society – *a church without walls*. When the Body of Christ is mobilized demonic agendas are obliterated, and God's strategic orders and purposes will permeated the Earth. In apostolic mobilization, God's troops, the saints, are sent out with a strategic mission to impact the kingdoms of this world and confiscate them for the Kingdom of our God.

Church, it is time to rise up and get our marching orders, because we are being mobilized!

> **"So, He said, "A nobleman went to a distant country to obtain for himself a kingdom, and [then] to return. So, he called ten of his servants, and gave them ten minas [one apiece, each equal to about a hundred days' wages] and said to them, 'Do business [with this] until I return."**
> **~ Luke 19:12-13**

Mobilization is God's end time assignment to evangelize the gospel on Earth. Whether it is the fivefold, the marketplace, or whatever sphere of influence we have been called to serve, we must never forget that the whole world is our pulpit.

In Mark 16:15, Jesus said, *"Go ye into all the world and preach the gospel!"* To preach or share the *"Good News"* in Greek is the words, *evgelion* or *evangelio*. These words are in reference to proclaiming the good news from one's appointed spheres. This is how the River of the Spirit will flow to all aspects of life and the mobilization of the body of Christ will affect the generations to come.

A Millennial Movement

"Behold, I will send you Elijah the prophet before the coming of the great and dreadful day of the LORD: And he shall turn the heart of the fathers to the children, and the heart of the children to their fathers, lest I come and smite the earth with a curse." ~ Malachi 4:5-6

Malachi was the last prophet under the governance of prophets. God did not speak to Israel until 400 years later. In the Old Testament, when the governing rule of prophets ended, an apostolic and prophetic people began to emerge in the age of the church. The spirit of Elijah has now come to turn the hearts of the fathers to the children. Sons and Daughters are beginning to embrace the Father's heart.

God is always after a generation! He is always pursuing a generation that can usher in His presence, power, and initiatives in the Earth realm.

Overall, the millennial movement is about the hearts of a generation turning back to the heart of God, so that the gospel can be mobilized, and His presence manifested on the Earth.

Western Culture and the Generation of Name-Giving[21]

The Baby Boomers
This nickname was given as a result of the increase of babies born following World War II.
1. Born between the years of 1946-1964
2. Age group ranging from 53-71 years old

Generation X
This name was given due to the low fertility rates following The "Baby Boom" era.
1. "The Baby Busters"
2. Born between the years of 1965-1980
3. Age group from 37-52 years old

---

[21] "American Generation Fast Facts," *CNN Online*, last modified November 11, 2013, https://www.cnn.com.

The Millennials

This generation is describes as the ones who are internet and technology savvy, they have been classified as superficial. Although society claims that there is no hope for them, they are the ones that God will raise up in the 3rd day awakening and will do exploits for His Kingdom.

1. Born between the years of 1980-2000
2. Age group ranging from 17-37 years old

"This is the generation of them that seek him, that seek thy face, O Jacob. Selah." ~ Psalms 24:6

Today, the cry for revival is being enthroned in the hearts of millennials around the world. God has always used a young generation to start revolutions and ignite revival fires. In fact, the greatest revival known to mankind started with a Jewish carpenter who was thirty years-old, who raised twelve disciples who turned the whole world upside down. As we know it today, Christianity is a result of their painstaking efforts to impact the globe with the gospel of Jesus Christ.

Throughout history, college students have come together in intense prayer. God has responded in great awakenings and released the spirit of revival. Generally, revivals come in times of great peril and darkness. God will use the desperate cry of the young as an end time compass that will show the way of the Lord, and they will carry the torch of revival.

In the coming days of glory global, we will see a

Greater intensity of evangelism on universities across the country. College campuses have become prayer grounds for missions and evangelism. For this reason, the coming generation of leaders is being developed right now on college and university campuses. Their passion and view of the world will impact the several mountains of society and impact the regions of the world.

The world is a controlled Anti-Christ system whose purpose is designed to rid the reality of God out of the consciousness of humanity. God will use a generation that will seek His face and they will play an important role in bringing glory global before Jesus' return.

Young glory carriers, will affect the nations, and will initiate the glory of God globally. Their assignment is to impact the world with the splendor of God. In *Matthew 28:19*, Jesus said, go ye and make disciples of nations. This is a clarion call to impact the regions of the world with the gospel of Jesus Christ. Today, many people around the world are still in darkness and have not experience the glorious light of life. For example, Japan has approximately one to three million Christians, which makes up only one percent of their population[22]. Although Buddhism is the leading religion, and the number of Christians in Japan appears to be very small in size, the impact and influence of Christianity has yet been great.

---

[22] "Christianity In Japan," New World Encyclopedia, accessed August 19, 2017. http://www.newworldencyclopedia.org/entry/Christianity_in_Japan.

I have been so privileged to pin a portion of this book in the nation of Japan and connect with believer's in that region of the world.

In *Matthew 5:14,* Jesus said we are the light of the world. As believers we have been called to fulfill the great commission. I am excited to see the gospel is advancing in the nation of Japan.

During the successive years, this planet has experienced great saturations of God's presence and spiritual awakenings, but there is yet something greater on the horizon. Although the Holy Spirit's objective for authenticity has been challenged by the traditions of men, there is yet a movement of last day glory carriers who are anticipating the third wave of glory which will come with greater force.

In the early moves of God, the Holy Spirit saturated regions of the world with His splendor, and people were Infused with God's mighty power. Many healing evangelists and missionaries went abroad in the Earth, and many people were filled with the baptism of the Holy Spirit. This was a great time that marked church history. However, there is a greater dimension and frequency of God's presence that is coming in the next wave of glory.

In the next wave of the glory, there will be great saturations of God's presence that will literally surpass the former moves of God. In all of this, the Holy Spirit's purpose will not just be charismatic renewal, but to restore the Kingdoms that were lost. These great saturations of the Spirit will come and will cause mighty impartations and activations of God's power and authority.

Listen to This Prophetic Forecast

The next move of God will bring a demonstration of God's power not only on the religious front, but also a grassroots movement on college campuses, the educational system, on political and economical fronts within business, sports and media arenas, etc. This next sovereign move of God will be a movement of believers who will arise and do exploits from their appointed spheres to advance God's Kingdom.

Charles Finney, the great theologian said:

"the simple idea of the Kingdom is that Christ Himself reigns in the hearts of his people, securing perfect submission of the will and consecration of every power to himself.[23]"

What the world is encountering right now is an emergence of an apostolic and prophetic people who are invading society! Business, government, education, media, sports, entertainment, religion, and family are literal kingdoms that are being confiscated and dominated for the Kingdom of our God.

---

[23] Charles Finney, "Seeking the Kingdom of God First," last modified August 27, 1845. https://www.gospeltruth.net.

In the midst of what looks bleak, God is yet raising up a people, and also churches, which will host the presence of God and function as miracle centers that will display His supernatural power with integrity.

In the early moves, people had more of a one-man focus, but the focus in the end time is one purpose with the objective to advance God's kingdom here on the Earth.

In spite of the obscurity of the hour and the issues of the local church, there is a generation that is rising up with a greater desperation for the presence of the living God to mobilize and maximize God's Kingdom, region by region and sphere by sphere.

> **"Say not ye, There are yet four months, and then cometh harvest? behold, I say unto you, Lift up your eyes, and look on the fields; for they are white already to harvest." ~ John 4:35**

Arise oh Bride; lift up your eyes the Bridegroom is coming. The former things are gone away behold the dawning of a new day. The Kingdom of God is moderately advancing. The Spirit of the Lord is crying out to humanity to leave their places of dormancy and restraint's and come into the threshold of the finest hour of the church age. The clarion call in this hour for Zion is to break the spirit of classism and develop an apostolic heritage that would awaken the nations. It's time to rise up and proclaim it from your appointed spheres! Zion has been called to a higher place, where the river is being restored!

Keys to Renewal

"And he said unto them, Go ye into all the world, and preach the gospel to every creature." Mark 16:15

The Kingdom of God functions as an embassy of Heaven. God's people are agents of His Kingdom. The church is more than a gathering place where people are religiously conformed. It is the place where people are being transformed and where they find their functionality in order to proclaim the gospel from their appointed spheres. Every believer should understand who they are as it relates to redemption, their relationship with God, and their position in His Kingdom for His service. In functionality, the believer understands how the kingdom functions and how they have been designed to function in it.

Highlights

Chapter Seven discloses the desire of God to saturate the planet with his presence. It reveals how the spirit of revival will come and encompass the earth in the third day awakening and wave of glory. We found out that the church functions at its highest level when it functions as God's Kingdom impacting the mountains that influence the society, the kingdoms of this world :

1. Business
2. Media
3. Entertainment
4. Education
5. Government
6. Religion
7. Family etc.

Transitional Prayer

"Anyone who believes in me may come and drink! For the Scriptures declare, 'Rivers of living water will flow from his heart." ~ John 7:38 NLT

Father, thank you for the quench of your Spirit and for the refreshing spring that is now flowing from my heart. May I ever long for you and never grow weary of pursuing you and reminded that you have already pursued me. May I Forever be consumed and captivated by you. Blessed be your glorious name forever; And may the whole earth be filled with your glory.
In Jesus' name, Amen!

Epilogue

The disarray and moral dysfunctions within our culture today will not be able to negate the next Great awakening that will bring a renewed reality of God's glorious presence to humanity. A church, city, or region of the world can never truly experience spiritual renewal, until it is first experienced through a people. When people are spiritually renewed and revived, they will become vessels that God will flow through to demonstrate His majestic power. Mysteries will be unveiled to those whose quest is for the most intimate path of righteousness. Wisdom is revealed in the face of the most Holy one. In the overflow of experiencing His presence, may you find the gaze of His beauty indescribable! I pray that this book has both challenged and inspired you to break the spirit of dormancy and religious cycles, so that the true and living God will manifest in your life and cause the Spirit of Revival to flow like a Mighty River from out of the inner chambers of your Heart.
May you never be the same!
In Jesus' Name!!

Bibliography

"American Generation Fast Facts." *CNN Online*. Last modified November 11, 2013. https://www.cnn.com.

Arnott, John. "The Toronto Blessing: What Is It?" last modified December 31, 1999. http://www.johnandcarol.org/updates/the-toronto-blessing-what-is-it.

"Avignon Papacy." *Encyclopedia Britannica*. Last modified December 31, 2014. https://www.britannica.com/event/Avignon-papacy.

Carr, Karen. "What Is A Proton? Atom and Chemistry" last modified June 2, 2017. http://quatr.us/chemistry/atoms/proton.htm.

Cartwright, Mark. "Narcissus" last modified February 20, 2017. https://www.ancient.eu/Narcissus/.

Cauchi, Tony. "Overview of The Healing Revival" last modified date September 2011. http://www.voiceofhealing.info.

"Census 2011: One-Third in Wales Have No Religion." *BBC News*. Last modified December 11, 2012. http://www.bbc.com/news/uk-wales-20678136.

"Christianity In Japan." New World Encyclopedia. Accessed August 19, 2017. http://www.newworldencyclopedia.org.

Christie, Vance "When Revival Came To Korea" last modified May 21, 2015. http://www.vancechristie.com/2015/05/21/when-revival-came-to-korea/.

Finney, Charles. "Seeking the Kingdom of God First." last modified August 27, 1845. https://www.gospeltruth.net.

Hall, Nancy. "Newton's First Law." last modified May 5, 2015. https://www.grc.nasa.gov/www/k-12/airplane/newton1.html.

"Honoring the Past." Brownsville Assembly of God. Accessed August 19, 2017. http://brownsville.church/about-us/history.

Kran, Brian and Wu, Brian "Blood Culture" last modified January 4, 2017. https://www.healthline.com/health/blood-culture#overview1.

"Martin Luther." *A & E Television Networks*. Last modified August 8, 2017, https://www.biography.com.

McMahon, T.C. "The Seeker-Friendly Way of Doing Church". March 2004. https://www.thebereancall.org.

Nordland, Rod. "A Welsh Teen Suicide Epidemic" last modified February 28, 2008. http://www.newsweek.com/welsh-teen-suicide-epidemic-94011.

"Religious Study Landscape." Accessed August 19, 2017. http://www.pewforum.org/religious-landscape-study/

"Evan Roberts." God's Generals. Accessed August 19, 2017. http://godsgenerals.com/evanroberts.

Severson, Lucky. "World's Biggest Congregation" last modified August 10, 2012. http://www.pbs.org/wnet/religionandethics/2012/08/10/august-10-2012-worlds-biggest-congregation/10162/.

"The Azusa Street Revival." Apostolic Archives International. Accessed August 19, 2017. http://www.apostolicarchives.com.

"Witchcraft Thriving In The Welsh Countryside." *Telegraph*. Last modified December 31, 2012. http://www.telegraph.co.uk

www.ingramcontent.com/pod-product-compliance
Lightning Source LLC
Chambersburg PA
CBHW070557160426
43199CB00014B/2537